THE RED LION

A Play in Three Acts

by Patrick Marber

‖SAMUEL FRENCH‖

samuelfrench.co.uk

FOR AMATEUR PRODUCTION ENQUIRIES

UNITED KINGDOM AND WORLD
EXCLUDING NORTH AMERICA
plays@samuelfrench.co.uk
020 7255 4302/01

Each title is subject to availability from Samuel French,
depending upon country of performance.

THINKING ABOUT PERFORMING A SHOW?

There are thousands of plays and musicals available to perform from Samuel French right now, and applying for a licence is easier and more affordable than you might think

From classic plays to brand new musicals, from monologues to epic dramas, there are shows for everyone.

Plays and musicals are protected by copyright law, so if you want to perform them, the first thing you'll need is a licence. This simple process helps support the playwright by ensuring they get paid for their work and means that you'll have the documents you need to stage the show in public.

Not all our shows are available to perform all the time, so it's important to check and apply for a licence before you start rehearsals or commit to doing the show.

LEARN MORE & FIND THOUSANDS OF SHOWS

Browse our full range of plays and musicals, and find out more about how to license a show

www.samuelfrench.co.uk/perform

Talk to the friendly experts in our Licensing team for advice on choosing a show and help with licensing

plays@samuelfrench.co.uk   020 7387 9373

Acting Editions

BORN TO PERFORM

Playscripts designed from the ground up to work the way you do in rehearsal, performance and study

---

Larger, clearer text for easier reading

Wider margins for notes

Performance features such as character and props lists, sound and lighting cues, and more

---

+ CHOOSE A SIZE AND STYLE TO SUIT YOU

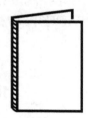

STANDARD EDITION

Our regular paperback book at our regular size

SPIRAL-BOUND EDITION

The same size as the Standard Edition, but with a sturdy, easy-to-fold, easy-to-hold spiral-bound spine

LARGE EDITION

A4 size and spiral bound, with larger text and a blank page for notes opposite every page of text – perfect for technical and directing use

MUSIC USE NOTE

Licensees are solely responsible for obtaining formal written permission from copyright owners to use copyrighted music in the performance of this play and are strongly cautioned to do so. If no such permission is obtained by the licensee, then the licensee must use only original music that the licensee owns and controls. Licensees are solely responsible and liable for all music clearances and shall indemnify the copyright owners of the play(s) and their licensing agent, Samuel French, against any costs, expenses, losses and liabilities arising from the use of music by licensees. Please contact the appropriate music licensing authority in your territory for the rights to any incidental music.

IMPORTANT BILLING AND CREDIT REQUIREMENTS

If you have obtained performance rights to this title, please refer to your licensing agreement for important billing and credit requirements.

ABOUT THE AUTHOR

Patrick Marber was born in London in 1964. He began his career as a writer in 1986. He co-wrote and appeared in a number of radio and television programmes including *The Day Today* and *Knowing Me, Knowing You*. In 1995 his first play, *Dealer's Choice*, premiered at the National Theatre in a production he also directed. Since then he has written plays and screenplays including *After Miss Julie, Closer, Howard Katz, Don Juan in Soho, The Red Lion, Hedda Gabler, Notes on a Scandal* and *Love You More*. He lives in London with his wife and their three children.

CHARACTERS

YATES – an old man
JORDAN – a young man
KIDD – somewhere in-between

SETTING

A semi-professional football club in the south of England.

The play is set in the home dressing room. The room is shabby but fit for purpose. It has been refurbished a few times since the late nineteenth century but there should be remnants of the past still present.

High ceiling, two windows overlooking the pitch. Rough linoleum floor. Long wooden benches. A line of iron hooks screwed into painted battens along each wall. A treatment table. A Belfast sink with a single brass tap. A small mirror over it. A low fridge.

A large built in storage cupboard. A small, square table with some papers on it. A white board. A cork notice board. A single bar electric heater mounted high on a wall – its orange glow.

A doorway leads off to an unseen bathroom with showers, WC and a single tub.

Elsewhere, a door leads to the outside. The door has an external sign fixed to it; the sign reads 'HOME'.

TIME

Three Saturdays in winter.
1. Noon.
2. Dusk.
3. Night.

The Red Lion was first performed in the Dorfman auditorium of the National Theatre, London on 3 June 2015. The cast and creatives were as follows:

YATES	Peter Wight
KIDD	Daniel Mays
JORDAN	Calvin Demba

Director	Ian Rickson
Designer	Anthony Ward
Lighting	Hugh Vanstone
Sound	Ian Dickinson
Music	Stephen Warbeck
Stage Manager	Joni Carter
Deputy Stage Manager	Maddy Grant
Assistant Stage Manager	Constance Oak
Staff Director	Anna Girvan

ONE

Noon. Winter.

A single bag on one of the benches. Above it a black trench coat on a hook.

Offstage, from the bathroom, sound of a shower running.

YATES *in his club tracksuit and trainers. His initials 'JY' in white letters on the track top. He is ironing. He takes a match day shirt from a laundry basket and irons it – inside out. Once the shirt is ironed he turns it right way round and kisses the badge. Then he puts the shirt on a hanger.*

During the act **YATES** *hangs each ironed shirt (sixteen in total) on separate hooks along the dressing room wall. Badge facing in. Number showing, '1' to '17' (but no '13' shirt).*

The shower stops running.

KIDD *enters from the bathroom. He wears flip-flops and a smart white bath robe with a hotel logo on the breast. A tube of shower gel in the pocket.*

He takes his mobile from the other pocket, checks a text message, curses briefly. Then sends a quick one back. Then he rubs out a player's name on the whiteboard.

KIDD *holds his hand out.* **YATES** *gives him a key and continues to iron.*

KIDD *opens a cupboard and takes out his suit. He takes it over to his bag on the bench and hangs the suit on a hook.* YATES *gestures and* KIDD *returns the key to him.*

KIDD *paces a bit – in thought – then he looks out the window from where he can see the pitch. He stares out.*

KIDD From up here...from *here*...you'd think it was emerald.

You get down *there*...it's a knackered old meadow.

It's not *true*. Divots. Tufts.

Can't play on that.

You can play. But you can't *play*.

Need it thick and short. Need it to *skim*.

KIDD *makes a skimming sound and motions with his hand. He stares out the window, shakes his head.*

He is sanding the goalmouth. He is sanding the bog he made himself.

Ken.

It's amateur.

Eh?

YATES *looks up.*

I talk to him, 'Hallo Ken, can you *help* me here? Can you give me a surface?'

He says he's on it. What's he on? He *mows* – does pretty stripes and circles – motors about, fat arse wedged in his 'ride on' mowing *tartan*. But he don't do the graft.

He needs to get out there with some *seed*. Chemicals! Fertilizer! Fuck knows – *he* should know!

Kenneth.

Eh?

YATES *stares at* KIDD.

You ever seen Ken with a fork? Have you ever seen him fork the pitch?

YATES He's a volunteer.

KIDD So?

YATES He's been groundsman fifteen years. Unpaid. Does it for love.

KIDD Can't he love the pitch a bit?

Pause.

YATES It's a plague pit. A burial ground. You got twenty thousand bodies under there.

KIDD Well I'm staggered it drains so well. 'Fact it drains *too* well'. It's rock on the flanks, do their hamstrings. Cheers, Ken, you dozy div!

KIDD *takes out a washbag and goes to the sink. He starts to brush his teeth.*

Loves a pint does Ken. A good old 'drink up'. In the club bar with the old soaks – the 'experts' – all yakking about formations: 'See at this level, I think the lads would be more *comfortable* with a fluid 4-4-2.'

'Oh, dead right, *Kenners*, you're spot on there.'

Fuckin' yard of ale.

KIDD *returns to the bench and starts to get dressed.*

What would help is if the pitch was used less. Yeah, great, 'Women's football.' 'The Ladies.'

YATES You ever watched 'em?

KIDD I'm busy Sunday mornings, see me kids.

KIDD *observes* YATES *working.*

You watch the Ladies?

YATES I watch all our teams.

KIDD You like the Ladies game?

YATES They're part of the Club.

KIDD They fuck the pitch! You got them, Youth team, Academy – you got the sponsors having a poncey kickabout and little kiddies pissing about in the goals – it mullers the turf!

YATES Community involvement.

KIDD It's unprofessional!

YATES We're non-league, Jim!

KIDD Yeah but we ain't a recreation ground! We ain't got *swings*. Ken let his dog on the pitch last week – big black Labrador bouncing about. How do I explain that to my players? Me an' Si and Rodge – we say train – prepare – think – conduct yourselves like *pros*. Oh – mind the dog shit.

YATES I'll talk to him.

KIDD If you would.

> **KIDD** *takes a tie out his jacket pocket. He unfurls it. It's badly creased. While* **YATES** *hangs another shirt up* **KIDD** *lays his tie on the ironing board.* **YATES** *returns to the ironing board, stops, sees the tie.*

YATES I'm doing the kit.

> *They face each other.*

KIDD It's a club tie. It's *kit*.

> **YATES** *thinks a moment then irons the tie.*

Obliged.

> **KIDD** *finishes dressing, puts on the tie, checks himself in the mirror. Spruces his hair. Then he goes to the white board, stares at his team.*

Roberts ain't coming. He's left the club.

YATES Ah.

KIDD Tosser texted me. He's gonna sign up the road. They poached him.

YATES Did Turner up his offer?

KIDD Shoved him another ton a week. I can't compete, I can't make the *moves* on this poxy budget.

YATES Robbo's class, he was always gonna go.

KIDD Get his kit back, yeah? Track suit, bag, training top – don't let him nick a fucking thread.

> **YATES** *nods.* **KIDD** *studies the white board.*

That kid.

> **YATES** *looks up.*

You rate him?

YATES Yeah.

KIDD Mmm. He *trains* well. He's a good little *trainer*. But out there...?

> **KIDD** *shrugs.* **YATES** *places a pair of neatly folded shorts and socks on the wooden bench below each shirt.*

YATES How are the kids?

KIDD Eh?

YATES Your children.

KIDD My *kids*?

YATES The ones you made.

KIDD How's *yours*? The fuck is that question?

YATES Innocent one.

KIDD No it ain't, not from *you*.

YATES Fuck off.

KIDD You fuck off.

YATES *continues his work.* KIDD *watches him.*

KIDD My kids are angry and confused. Alright?

KIDD *paces, restlessly.*

She wants a divorce. 'It don't work. Not for me, personally.' *Personally.*

YATES You said that?

KIDD No, Karen. 'There is a world where this works. But this ain't that world.'

YATES It never is.

KIDD Two years time you're in the street, see some guy holding hands with your kids, buying them ice cream. You approach, 'Oh. Hallo'. They look at you strange. You know?

YATES *(softly)* Yeah.

YATES *starts to sweep the floor.* KIDD *walks around, finds a bit of rubbish, kicks it towards the pile* YATES *is making.*

KIDD She's gone *legal.* She's killing me. I got nowhere to go. I'm kippin on carpets. Phone provider says they're gonna chop me off. *(Takes out his phone)* I lose this I lose my – my wherewithal. It's a *limb.* I say, 'I *need* it, it's how I conduct my business.'

YATES Can't you... 'pay as you go'?

KIDD Eh??

YATES Isn't it a thing...?

KIDD It's for infants and drug dealers. And my former employers – that horrible club – them owners – them millionaire *brewers.* They owe me sixteen grand compensation. Owed it me near three years.

YATES I know.

KIDD They say, 'Be patient.' I wait. 'Be patient, feller, it's coming.' I wait. 'I really need it guys.' It ain't coming. And now it turns

out they're filing for administration. They done me, John.
Did me like a child. Sixteen grand. I'll *get* it but they'll settle
on the drip when what I need is the *lump*. They *promised*.
Formal handshake. I trusted 'em cos they were proper, cos
they spoke nice. What good is a man's word if it's just a
fucking sound he makes?

YATES You got debts, Jimmy?

KIDD Who hasn't? Four kids don't need some deadbeat father.
I ain't cryin about it. I'm just tellin' you. I could do with
some *flow*.

YATES Ask the Board for a loan.

KIDD I did. I'm good for it, John. If you got a bit put by? Some
nest egg...? I'm asking you.

They look at each other.

YATES I'm scraping to pay the rent.

KIDD *looks away, in despair.* YATES *has finished
sweeping. He puts the broom back in the cupboard and
takes out a dustpan and brush. He kneels down to the
small pile he's made on the floor and gets to work.*

KIDD Go on then; today's officials.

YATES Mr Parker, Mr Langley, Mr Sengupta.

KIDD Oh, Mr Parker. 'It is He Who Cannot See.'

YATES 'He Is The Poor Blind Referee.'

KIDD Yet the man's *hearing* is uncanny. He sent me off, four years
back. 'Salty language'. Trophy game out East. One of theirs
does one of ours. Rakes him. Achilles. Old school. Parker
whistles, gives the free kick to *them*! Our lad's stretchered
off. I'm in the dug out. I murmur. I *whisper*: 'You cheat,
you blind fucking prick.' Ref's full thirty yards up the pitch.
Turns. Straight red. I almost applauded his sensory powers.
'Mr Kidd, I must ask you to leave the playing arena.' *Arena.*
Their main stand is a cattle shed. It's chucking it down.
Horizontal. I hunch the touchline. Sueders sinking in the

mud. Whole ground hating on me. Three hundred pig farmers singing 'Fuck off' in various melodies. I show no fear – *(Sticks his chest out)* – I'm full robin red breast. To get out you gotta pass this area – this *latrine* they call a 'Family Enclosure'. Them lot are the *worst*; all the pubey lads givin' it large, 'Wanker, Wanker.' Some pikey bint fights her way to the front – she gobs on me. She spits on my sleeve! Fucking flob. I keep my shape, politely offer the finger – at which this grandad hurls his pie. I duck, he bellows, 'You gay cunt.' Whole families cheering him on. Yeah, I remember Mr Parker. You got his biscuits?

YATES Rich tea.

KIDD I thought he liked a ginger?

YATES He used to. He's moved on.

KIDD Ooh, you're good!

YATES It's in the details.

KIDD You and your biscuit spreadsheet. And where's the *harm*?

YATES The man is human.

KIDD He's a human being.

YATES Or so he manifests.

KIDD And if he should unconsciously *favour* us, who's to know of our marginal gain?

YATES We will serve him the biscuit he likes.

KIDD Why serve him the biscuit he does not like?

YATES We're hospitable people.

KIDD It's not a *bribe*.

YATES It's a courtesy.

KIDD The incremental edge.

YATES Proud tradition of the club.

They chuckle. KIDD *studies his team on the white board.*

KIDD Prediction?

YATES Three one, home win.

KIDD We could go third.

YATES Be good.

KIDD Keep this going, we're right in it.

> **KIDD** *studies the white board again.*

You reckon that kid?

YATES Yep.

KIDD Yeah?

YATES Decent.

KIDD The *pace* on him. The touch. The *caress*.

YATES He's coming early. Due now.

KIDD Yeah?

YATES He was a bit tight after training, I said he could have a rub.

KIDD New favourite?

YATES He's a good kid.

> **YATES** *puts the ironing board away. He gives the treatment table a wipe, takes out some massage lotions and oils from the cupboard.*

KIDD When he comes, gimme five.

> **YATES** *nods.*

You reckon he's ready?

YATES Yeah.

KIDD Without the loyal 'Robbo' we got room on the bench. Kid won't crumble out there?

YATES Nah.

JORDAN *appears at the door, carrying his kit bag.*

JORDAN Shall I come back?

KIDD No, come in!

YATES Alright?

JORDAN Yeah.

YATES *exits.* **JORDAN** *looks confused.*

KIDD He's coming back.

JORDAN *stands, a bit awkward.*

You can put that on there.

JORDAN *puts his bag on the bench.* **KIDD** *sizes him up.*

I been impressed with you. New club, don't know us, learning our *ways*. Kept your head down, bit quiet but good ethic. And you don't moan. No one likes a moaner. But I gotta be frank; I'm not feeling the *passion*. You wanna have a *kickabout* there's pub teams. Play five a side down the leisure centre. This ain't that.

JORDAN I wanna play, Boss.

KIDD You wanna play here?

JORDAN Yes, Boss.

KIDD You wanna play for me?

JORDAN Yes.

KIDD Can you be loyal? Because I am demanding. I'm a prickly prick of a person. I'm a bad loser. Losing is an insult. I hate it, I fear it, I dread its dreadful meaning. And when I lose I don't do it graceful. I *howl*. I kick a puppy. I'll kick *you*. You'll think I hate you but I don't. I hate the part of you who's defeated. I hate the in-bred piece of you thinks losing's your birthright. You understand?

JORDAN Yes.

KIDD To *win*. What a lovely word. It brings us to rest: 'Win.' The will to win. You got that? The guts, do the necessary?

JORDAN Yes, Boss.

KIDD Men die out there. I saw it once.

> **KIDD** *stares at* **JORDAN**.

Tell me about your left knee. You protect it. And you do it very clever. Took me an' Si a few sessions to suss it.

> *Pause.*

JORDAN I was injured.

KIDD Yes. When?

JORDAN I was fourteen.

KIDD Ligaments? Cruciate? What?

> *Pause.*

JORDAN A man with a baseball bat.

KIDD Hmm. Why d'he do that?

JORDAN He didn't like me. But it's healed. It was all busted up but now it's healed.

> **KIDD** *stares at* **JORDAN**.

KIDD Thing is, you say a thing you don't believe. You can't play you don't trust yourself – trust you're *strong*. Cos all you are – out *there* – all you are is everything you got.

Some cunt gives you a smack. In the past.

And I know those men. I really do.

But you ain't no use less you brave. No use at all.

> **KIDD** *looks* **JORDAN** *in the eye.* **JORDAN** *might be about to cry.*

Don't blub. This ain't the place. You keep it together.

JORDAN Yeah.

KIDD Alright?

JORDAN Yeah.

KIDD Good boy. You strong?

JORDAN I won't let you down.

KIDD No you won't. I'm gonna start you on the bench.

JORDAN Thanks, Boss!

KIDD We're over budget. If you get on I'll slip you thirty quid – call it expenses.

JORDAN ...OK.

KIDD Out my pocket. Don't tell *no one*. Me and you.

> **KIDD** *stares at* **JORDAN** *until he nods his assent.*

> You *dazzle*. Then we can talk about a little wage. Legit, through the books. Maybe even a contract. You fancy that?

JORDAN Yes, Boss, I'd like that.

KIDD Goodo. Take the '17'.

> **JORDAN** *approaches the '17' shirt. Stops.*

JORDAN Can I wear the '14'?

KIDD Don't be silly.

JORDAN I like that number.

KIDD It's not on offer!

JORDAN Please. I had a vision. Last night. I saw myself in the '14'.

KIDD Is this a religious thing or a drug thing?

JORDAN Religious.

KIDD You – what – muslim or something?

JORDAN I'm a Christian.

KIDD Jesus Christ wore '14'? Oh, I offend you?

JORDAN *Yes.*

KIDD Get over it.

JORDAN (*forcefully*) I believe, Boss. You don't like it thass alright but I believe in God and I love him.

KIDD Where you trot off on a Sunday is not my biz. But *here*, you're in *my* chapel. Have you got a problem with authority?

JORDAN Yeah.

KIDD Yeah what?

JORDAN *Boss*.

KIDD Is it a long term problem?

JORDAN I think it might be.

KIDD Well, I got the same. Whoever got some hold over me, I wanna kill. But needs must. *Eh?*

JORDAN nods. Looks down. KIDD lifts the boy's chin, gently.

They are close. KIDD looks him in the eye.

Were you unruly?

JORDAN nods.

You get caught?

JORDAN nods.

KIDD They lock you up?

After a while, JORDAN nods. KIDD holds his look. Keeps his chin up.

'S'alright. We've all offended. The state is not your mate. They hate us. But in here...it's a jolly old pirate ship. Eh?

JORDAN nods.

We're gonna win this league. And we're gonna better ourselves. And we will be blessed. (*Softly*) Something like grace.

KIDD *hands* **JORDAN** *the '17' shirt.*

KIDD There you go, well done.

JORDAN Thanks, Boss.

KIDD Don't thank me, you earned it.

YATES *comes in, carrying twenty match day programmes.*

YATES *(To* **KIDD***)* Si wants you. He's setting out the cones.

KIDD You sort this boy? He made the squad.

KIDD *exits.* **JORDAN** *grins at* **YATES***.*

YATES Good lad.

JORDAN *holds up his shirt, showing the number.*

It's a fine number. It's a prime number.

YATES *goes to his cupboard and rummages around for some kit.*

JORDAN *takes out his phone, starts to text.*

JORDAN Texting my mum.

YATES Want me to get her some tickets? Players perk.

JORDAN Nah. She won't come. She don't approve. She thinks you're very bad men.

YATES She's right.

JORDAN *(shrugs)* She don't know a good man from a bad.

YATES *has found a club tracksuit and kit bag. He gives them to* **JORDAN***.*

YATES You wear this every training session and match day. You forget to wear it, you're fined a tenner. You lose it, I'll fine you fifty quid. If you leave the club you return it. Laundered.

YATES *places a match day programme on each player's spot on the benches.* JORDAN *watches, enjoying* YATES*'s precision, his quiet concentration.*

JORDAN I prayed last night. I prayed for this.

YATES There is a God.

JORDAN There really is.

You looked out for me, these weeks. Kept me honest. You're a good man, they all say it.

YATES I have a reputation.

JORDAN 'Ledge'.

YATES Hmm.

JORDAN Don't like praise?

YATES I like it too much.

YATES *taps the treatment table.*

And I don't like the word, 'Legend'. It's bollocks. The *club* is the legend.

JORDAN *starts taking his clothes off.* YATES *goes to the cupboard and takes out some towels, arranges them on the treatment table.*

JORDAN The boys said you played here. Way back.

Pause. YATES *looks at* JORDAN.

YATES Yeah. I wore the '5'.

JORDAN You any good?

YATES You'd know I was there.

JORDAN *looks at* YATES, *still curious.*

JORDAN They said you built the North Stand.

YATES Nah. I played in a game which built it. A couple of years after the Battle of Hastings. And bloody in its way.

JORDAN Yeah?

YATES FA Cup tie. We'd scraped through to first round proper. We're playing a team three leagues above us. The game is bigger than Christmas. 'Bout twenny minutes from time one of theirs knees me in the mush. Intentional but ref doesn't see. I'm staggering. Eyes, nose, gob. *Whoosh*. Only blood. A tooth in my palm. Ref's looking at me, 'Are you sure, son'. Our bench gestures me come off but we've already used our sub. *(Softly, remembering)* My wife's there...she... her hand on her mouth. Other arm...she's holding our first born. Our girl...a little bundle in a red shawl... It's nil nil, it's *snowing*. They're killing us – fitter, stronger – we're pegged in, defending our lives. Five to go – some miracle we nick a corner. Boss waves, 'Get up there, boy. Gooo onnn.' I go plodding. I'm *dead*. Pitch is glue. You know? Ball comes over from the corner. A brown bomb. Low and hard. Near post. I dive to this blur, eyes of blood, catch it sweet. *Boof*. Get in. Thing flies so fast no one sees it 'til the crowd *roars*. I'm on my front, whole team pile on, kissing me, squeezing my nuts, pitch invasion, all the trimmings. *(Softly)* That day... I was never so loved.

Next round we got lucky: away draw in the North East – huge club. We took 3,000 up there. I couldn't play, turns out I'd fractured my jaw. But this game; we got half a massive gate. On the telly. Made this club rich a moment. We lost eight nil.

JORDAN Was it in colour?

YATES The world? It seemed to be. So they built that stand. And still it stands. And it's a good one. But I didn't build it. I did help my Dad do some of the electrics.

YATES *points to the treatment table.*

Jump up.

JORDAN *is stripped to his underwear.*

JORDAN Erm...?

He gestures to his pants.

YATES As you are or as you were born.

JORDAN Are you a qualified masseur?

YATES Over the last half century, I've seen a thousand penises in here; from the dainty to the dumbfounding. I think I can cope.

JORDAN gets on the table wearing his underpants. YATES starts the massage – back and legs.

Alright?

JORDAN Yeah. Thanks.

YATES puts more oil on his hands, works it in.

YATES OK?

JORDAN Yeah.

YATES works on the shoulders.

YATES Tension.

JORDAN Mmm.

YATES Can't play if you're coiled. Gotta be loose.

JORDAN Guy said it me when I was sixteen. 'Unclench the fist. Unload the gun.'

YATES Literally?

JORDAN Nah. He was a...like a therapist.

YATES Uh huh. Where?

JORDAN In this place for very tense kids.

YATES To be good, good at anything, you gotta be tight. But to be *great,* you gotta loosen up. We shall trick you into a state of nonchalance.

YATES *continues the massage. Thinks. Lowers his voice...*

I was gonna say...if you wanted someone...for advice. Guidance. I'm here... I'm *around*. Kid like you. A prospect. Word travels. They descend: Agents. Scouts. Managers. You know? I could protect you. Deal with those situations. Look after your interests...

JORDAN Be my agent?

YATES No. I – I'd just be a feller...who's there for you.

They look at each other.

Don't need to tell anyone. Best not to.

JORDAN I dunno if I want the complication, you know?

YATES Yeah.

JORDAN Nothing personal.

YATES Yeah.

YATES *continues the massage, furious with himself.*

After a while KIDD *bustles in and addresses* JORDAN.

KIDD A thing. Shoulda said. A word about the officials at this level of the pyramid: a man who can lodge a small pencil in the top of his sock and then jog about without dislodging it is a qualified referee. He is scared and helpless, a baby in black. He needs to be shown the way. This league you gotta be *canny*. We must help the man in black to *see*. We must lead the poor blind soul through this overwhelming universe. You get?

JORDAN ...No, Boss.

KIDD You get on today, some big bully kicks you – you exclaim, you go down, you show you're *hurt* – because you *are*. You get in the box – you feel a nibble, a brush, you sense a presence, you imagine 'contact', you *tumble*. Do it subtle, no leaping, no one shot you, you ain't no *gazelle*.

YATES *eases off on the massage.*

Throw ins, fouls, offsides, corners – any decision the ref gotta make, you claim for *us*. Make him *think* for *us*. He's lost, you beckon him to the truth – as we define it. There it is.

KIDD *makes to exit.*

JORDAN I won't cheat.

KIDD *stops, turns.*

I don't *cheat*.

KIDD It's a *team* game!

JORDAN I know.

KIDD Team fuckin' game, kid!

JORDAN I know that!

YATES *quietly slips over to the sink, rinses his hands. Watches.*

KIDD Can't play a lad does his own selfish thing.

JORDAN I won't dive.

KIDD These *words*!

JORDAN I'm not a cheat.

KIDD Did I ask you to?

JORDAN No.

KIDD Did I use that word?

JORDAN No.

KIDD So?

JORDAN Sorry.

KIDD What I encouraged you to do was to apply game intelligence.

JORDAN Can I...?

KIDD Can you think about it? No. You step up or fuck off. Right now.

Silence. **JORDAN** *gets off the treatment table and hands* **KIDD** *the '17' shirt.*

KIDD Thass a shame.

JORDAN Sorry.

KIDD Uh huh.

Now **JORDAN** *sadly offers* **YATES** *the club track suit and kit bag.*

YATES *makes a slight move but* **KIDD** *glances at him,* **YATES** *stays put.*

JORDAN *starts to put his own clothes on. Track bottoms, a sweat shirt.*

KIDD You reckon yourself? Too super talented to play non-league?

JORDAN No.

KIDD You might be half decent but you ain't the bollocks, boy. You wouldn't be *here* if you were. But there is a road *out* of here; you play for me – play *with* me – I will show you to some *glory*. I can change your life. This is a step to another step up.

JORDAN *(passionately)* I won't cheat, I won't lie, I won't *fake*. Not for you, not for no one! I mean to *stand* for something – you got it, Mister? All my life they tell me what to think and to feel and to do but no one – *no one* knows what I feel – sometimes *I* don't know! You don't get to mess in this maze I got. You ain't my father – you ain't my boss – you got nothing I need. Show me *beauty* – give me what's true and tender and real. You don't get to play with my morals just cos I wanna play. Fuck you and your slyness. Don't tell me to be strong – GIVE ME SOME STRENGTH!

KIDD OK. One: No, not my job, you find it in *you*. Two: Chill the fuck out. Three: Shut the fuck up and Four: Listen: We are *winning*! Eight games unbeaten – I've built a miracle – a winning *team* – and I'm picking *you*! Cos me, Si, Rodge, Yatesy – *my* team – we've noticed you can kick a ball about in a delightful fashion. We think you have heart and intelligence. We believe you might be a *footballer*. A *real* one. We talk about kids like you and we gurgle with joy. In three hours time a contest will be staged out there. Seven hundred people will pay cash money to observe a spectacle of aggression, technique and guile. BE IN IT!!! You know that word?

JORDAN I know that word.

KIDD The word 'guile'.

JORDAN I know it!

KIDD So get involved! *Belong*! Do what I say: play for the team, earn what is our due, win the game. Our supporters – this club – your *team* – they will *love* you – if you let them. Don't be the fuck up! Be the one who makes it through. You're gonna say 'yes' so let's not drag it out.

> *JORDAN glances at* YATES *who remains inscrutable. Then* JORDAN *looks at* KIDD.

JORDAN Alright.

KIDD Good lad.

JORDAN Yeah.

KIDD We're good.

> *They shake hands.* KIDD *raises his eyebrows to* YATES *and exits.*

JORDAN Did you cheat?

YATES I cheated, I lied and I conned anyone I could. I terrorised the young, kicked shit out the old. And I went looking for it. In my defence, I was a deranged young man. Five years we were the best team in this district. We were hooligans. On the park, on the piss, home, away. Up the high road. We were *kings*. But *you*...don't lower yourself. Don't do a thing you don't believe in. You're different class, boy.

> YATES *holds his look, lets* JORDAN *settle a moment and then taps the treatment table.*

JORDAN   You know this man...

YATES   Jimmy.

JORDAN   Is he all that?

YATES   I work for him. He's my boss.

JORDAN   I saw a picture down in that bar. You *were* the boss.

YATES   Twenty years ago. For two seasons.

> JORDAN *removes his clothes, climbs back on the treatment table.*

I took us down. Lowest points total in the club's history. People who loved me couldn't look at me. Took me ten years to show my face again...

> YATES *continues the massage.*

All that season, in here: 'Do this, track this one, you tuck in if he goes.'

'We can get out of this, lads. We won't be *relegated*. Believe, boys, *believe*!'

And other horseshit from the same yard.

'Keep going, lads, keep going'. I'd do this:

> YATES *makes a gesture of energy and uplift.*

They look away. Don't believe in you. Why should they?

To lose them...like drowning...and lose yourself.

You're an old fool. You're the plague.

JORDAN   You gonna answer my question?

YATES Jimmy Kidd knows how to win. Don't need to agree with the man to be on his team. In this room: *loyalty*. Rest of the world go fuck itself.

YATES *continues the massage in silence.*

JORDAN The boys said you played pro.

YATES Old Division 3.

JORDAN Yeah?

YATES For two seasons. Loved it.

But I was a journeyman. All heart...no touch.

I ended up here. Dug in.

My dad played years for this club. County league days.

He could play a bit...

I used to come in here half time, eight years old, bring the oranges...

Those men. Giants. All hair and cock and laughter.

The pips and peel on my plate.

'Thanks, kid.'

Terrified.

Longing for their approval. To be those men.

Their secrets...

And the holy reek of them: sweat and liniment and dubbin.

Fags and talc and booze.

'Alright, John Junior.'

To be the kid...

To *play*...

(nods) That's my peg.

My father said a football man dies three times:

Once when he's young and sees he's only second rate.

Twice when he hangs up his boots and has to live like the others.

And the third time...slow...if he falls out of love with the game.

YATES *continues the massage.*

OK?

JORDAN *(slight pain)* Mmm.

YATES Here?

JORDAN Lower.

YATES *(of the knee)* Bit swollen.

JORDAN S'alright.

YATES *continues in silence. Finally, he taps* JORDAN.

YATES You're done. You warm up good and strong. Keep these loose.

YATES *goes to the sink, washes his hands.*

JORDAN Reckon I'll get on?

YATES You might. I'll nudge him.

JORDAN Can I tell you something?

YATES The kit man is a priest, you tell him anything.

JORDAN I'm scared.

YATES Be insane if you weren't.

JORDAN My heart's burning and bumping.

YATES *stills him, gently.*

YATES Adrenaline. It's alright. You're safe.

YATES *holds him a moment.* JORDAN *calms. Looks at* YATES.

JORDAN He's paying me. Said he'd find me thirty quid. He said don't tell no one. Call it expenses. Thass not right. Is it?

YATES What else d'he say?

JORDAN He banged on about losing. Bit fuckin out there, you know?

YATES Oh yeah. He's that. Styles himself a maverick. Likes a *preen.* He lives for the cameras. But round here, they are scarce.

JORDAN *gets up from the treatment table, stretches a bit.* **YATES** *puts the towels in a laundry basket, the massage oils back in his cupboard.*

They'll be coming in. Soon enough.

JORDAN *starts putting his kit on.* **YATES** *takes out the warm up tops, hangs one on each hook.* **JORDAN** *watches him, intently.*

JORDAN What's your cut?

YATES Eh?

JORDAN Before. Thing you said. What would you *take*?

YATES *shakes his head.*

Everyone wants a cut.

YATES I don't.

JORDAN ...You...?

YATES No.

JORDAN No take?

YATES No. I'd...you know...

JORDAN You'd...?

YATES Yeah.

JORDAN You'd do it for love?

YATES The honour. I believe in you.

JORDAN You'll look after me?

YATES Yes.

> *Pause.*

JORDAN You got a deal, mister.

> **JORDAN** *offers his hand,* **YATES** *shakes it.*

Home team.

> **JORDAN** *hugs* **YATES**. **YATES** *is overcome.*

Thanks, Boss.

YATES Easy. Jim's the boss.

> **JORDAN** *gets his boots out, starts to loosen the laces.*

What are those?

JORDAN Shit boots. You gonna get me a sponsor?

YATES When you play like a young God.

> **JORDAN** *watches* **YATES**. *Thinks. Flexes his leg. Wants to tell him something.*

Don't take his money.

JORDAN It's thirty quid.

YATES When he comes to pay you, say you can't take it.

JORDAN Why?

YATES Principle. The club should pay you, not him. Keep it *clean.*

JORDAN Alright.

YATES Let him know who you are.

JORDAN Who I am is broke.

> **YATES** *offers* **JORDAN** *a twenty pound note. And then a ten.*

No – I wasn't asking – I can't.

YATES I'm a billionaire. Pay me back when you're flush.

JORDAN *nods, takes the cash.*

JORDAN Thank you.

YATES *goes to his cupboard, takes out a mop and a packet of Rich Tea biscuits.*

YATES Ref's due. I gotta slop out his lair. Keep them limbs nice and easy.

JORDAN Always loose.

Pause. They look at each other.

YATES See you on the park.

YATES *exits.*

JORDAN *sits back on the bench, luxuriating a moment.*

Then he goes to the window. Looks out.

He returns to the bench and unzips a pocket in his bag.

He pulls out a syringe and loads it from a small phial.

He straightens his left leg.

Then he injects himself just above the knee.

TWO

Dusk. Six weeks later.

Heavy rain.

After the match. Dirty kit on the floor. Empty plastic bottles. Shin pads. Sock tape.

Bandages. Mud. A subs board.

KIDD *enters – black trench coat over his suit. He wears a fedora.*

He quickly looks around then hurries into the bathroom. He comes back out and takes out his phone. A cheaper phone than the one he had before. **KIDD** *makes a call.*

KIDD *(in phone)* Mac? Jim. It's a new num – no, keep the old – I'm between *providers*. Between – yeah. I'm talking to him now! He's standing right next to me!

YATES *hurries in, huddled, coat over his tracksuit. Soaked and cold.*

KIDD *immediately exits to the bathroom, still talking.*

(in phone, exiting) Yeah – all over it – I know – yeh yeh yeh.

YATES *opens his coat and takes out the pint he's been protecting and a wrapped bag of chips with a saveloy. He puts them on the table. He takes off his coat, shakes it out, hangs it up.* **YATES** *takes a glug of his bitter. Then he stands on a bench, reaches up, warms his hands on the wall mounted heater. He contemplates the room*

and the work he must now do. He opens his chips. Eats.
Drinks. YATES *has the pint in his hand as* KIDD *comes*
in from the bathroom.

YATES Guilty.

YATES *puts the glass down.*

KIDD How many times? Place – of – work. Oh. Enjoy your
bloody pint.

YATES *drinks.*

You seen the kid?

YATES In the office. He's having a chat with *The Herald.*

KIDD He's doing *press?*

YATES Charlie H wanted an interview. Man of the match. Want
some?

KIDD Reckon he'll be long?

YATES Ten minutes.

KIDD *takes a few chips. Paces.* YATES *goes to his cupboard,*
takes out ketchup, adds it to his chips. KIDD *takes his*
hat off. Shakes it. Carefully brushes it down.

KIDD Do I look a tit?

KIDD *puts the hat back on.*

YATES Twirl.

KIDD *does so.*

You look immense.

KIDD *puts his hat on a hook.* YATES *starts to tidy the*
room. This will occupy him throughout the act. He starts
by sorting the wet, muddy kit into three baskets – shirts
(all turned inside out), socks, shorts. KIDD *takes his*
coat off, shakes it out, hangs it up. Warms his hands.

KIDD I'll have a bath. You stick the immersion on?

YATES *exits to the bathroom.*

What a super game of semi-professional football!

YATES *(offstage)* Yeah!

KIDD Oh, my former club. Them brewers. *(Addresses the white board)* Enjoy the spanking, did ya? Enjoy your education by a tactical *maestro*? Heh heh. *(Calls off)* I hate to gloat but tell me I was *regal* out there?

Pause.

Yatesy?

YATES *(offstage)* You were regal!

KIDD We buried 'em, we funeraled the fuckers. Ha ha!

KIDD *takes a can of Diet Coke from the fridge.*

YATES *(re-entering)* I had a drink with their kit-man, even he said we're playing some.

KIDD Oh we're playing *symphonic*. Feel it.

They both feel it a few seconds. Then KIDD *turns to* YATES, *significantly.*

YATES No, Jim!

KIDD Whadidisay? Did I speak?

YATES It's a 'no' Jim.

KIDD Come *on*! You saw him play today? Did you see him, the cherub who bossed the game?

YATES Yeah.

KIDD You saw?

YATES *Yes.*

KIDD You say you saw but did you *see*?

YATES I was in the fucking dug out, of course I *saw*!

KIDD But did you see? Can you still *see*?

YATES I can see!

KIDD Talent. Temperament. Timing.

YATES Is that from a book?

KIDD He's a ghost! He finds space that ain't there, he's so fucking good he don't exist! He's a young – a young – a young –

YATES Too soon to say, let him *breathe*!

KIDD Ooh, he's a Prince.

YATES He's just a *kid*!

KIDD We knew he was good but this one's a *peach*. Tell me he's mustard, tell me this kid is *outstanding*. Say what you say, Ledge. Say that lovely thing you say.

    Pause.

YATES He can play.

KIDD There it is! He Can Play. Eh? Can't he? Ha ha!!! Say it again.

YATES *(smiles)* He can play.

KIDD He – Can – Play! How *much* can he play, John?

YATES I said he can play.

KIDD So help me get him to sign his *contract*! We gotta find him more money! Now saddle the fuck up to the Board and argue the *case*!

YATES I went last week! They said no!

KIDD You have to ask *again* – have to, *have* to – irresponsible not to! My job – my profession – my *calling*, feller – my holy moly *creed*.

YATES I respect your bubbly enthusiasm – now fuck off.

KIDD *exclaims with frustration.*

YATES Your current overspend is more than a grand a week!

KIDD It's frontloaded – front the fuck loaded – I'm asking a ton more a week to sign the new *Pele*!

YATES 'New Pele.'

KIDD Shorthand. Fuck your mockery.

YATES You wanna increase the offer you'll have to *juggle*. Board won't sanction a penny more.

KIDD 'Sanction'? Who *are* you?!

YATES There's no more money! You spent it and then you spent the overspend!

KIDD Fuckin' Dennis out there.

YATES I saw you haranguing.

KIDD Fuckin' Dennis, fuckin' cock.

YATES I don't disagree.

KIDD 'What d'you reckon,' I say. 'What about that beautiful, glorious kid, eh?' Dennis goes, 'Mmm. I can see the logic, but I don't think the Board'll go for it.' I say, 'Yes but Mr Club Secretary, *you've* watched the boy play these last weeks, you've seen what he can *do*, player like that is an *asset*, he should be *ours*, we gotta lock him down on contract so them vultures up the road can't steal him! A wise football man like yourself, you who have the ear of our distinguished Board –' He chuckles. He fuckin' *chuckles*, Ledge.

YATES Maybe he saw through you?

KIDD D'you know I think he might. So let's explore another universe –

YATES I live in this one!

KIDD And it's a sorry one cos you live in fear! Fuck the Board, fuck the Board, fuck, fuck, fuck the Board! You were a *rogue*, you know how it's *done* – 'sanction'?! Them and Us. Since

Time Began. John: Be – With – Us! Now *you* gotta talk to the Board, *you* gotta tell 'em to release the cash – I've tried but they don't seem to like me – it's *baffling*. But you they respect, from *you* they will *listen*!

YATES They don't listen, they humour me!

KIDD You're the *king* – power behind the throne!

YATES The king *is* the fucking throne!

KIDD Why are you so reluctant to do what you know is *right*?!

KIDD *shakes his head.*

It's a frickin' mystery. Three weeks back: 'Here you go, son. Here's the dream, sign there.' 'Can I think about it?' 'Course you can but think it quick, eh?' He's *still* thinking! It don't stack up.

KIDD *paces in frustration then turns.*

Someone's got to him.

YATES *holds his look.*

It's them up the road, that stinking rotten club. *Turner*. First he poached Roberts and now he's gonna poach our boy. They've tapped him up.

YATES Nah.

KIDD No?

YATES How would they get to him?

KIDD Carrier pigeon. Fuck should I know? They induced him with a can of Sprite down the discotheque. They smuggled a painted lady into his humble lodgings. Or maybe they *phoned* him?

YATES Nah. Kid wouldn't sign for them.

KIDD And you know this *how*? Some optimistic fucking whimsy?

YATES He's loyal, he loves it here.

KIDD So why won't he sign?! Them up the road are a league above us and they'll double his wage. Your mate Turner's a crafty old cove, I bet he puts in a seven dayer, first thing Monday. Then we're fucked! Thass why I been begging the Board, 'Get this kid on contract, protect ourselves.' And no one *listens* cos no one believes a thing happens til it *does*. No faith in the manager. When will someone in this world believe in me?! John, go see the Board – they're in there now!

YATES I've been! I told you! THEY SAID NO!

KIDD stares at YATES a moment. YATES continues to tidy up. KIDD checks his phone, quickly responds to a text.

KIDD Long interview. Can't we fish him out?

KIDD looks at JORDAN's hook, his club kit bag on the bench. KIDD approaches.

YATES Oi.

KIDD I'm looking for the contract.

YATES Don't touch his stuff.

KIDD Alright. Keep your knickers on.

KIDD paces. YATES watches him.

YATES You want me to talk to him?

KIDD He ain't gonna listen to *you* – he plays for *me*.

YATES continues to clear up. KIDD watches him a while.

KIDD goes to the window.

The pitch. One floodlight still on.

My sweet Lord. He's forking the pitch. Ken has got his fork out.

YATES I had a word.

KIDD There it is: Influence.

KIDD *has a thought, looks at* YATES, *dismisses the thought.*

KIDD *goes and lies on the treatment table while* YATES *works.*

Did you see the pass for the second goal? Outside of the boot – wrong foot – does he have a wrong foot? Fifty yards? Sixty? *Boooom.* Have you *ever*? On this quagmire? Ever? In space, behind the 3, in his back pocket. Defender almost dies the ball's so snide. It hangs – hovers – *plummets.* Their keeper goes 'Waaagghh' – he *wets* his goal mouth. Benno don't break stride – even *he* can't miss! They don't run to him, they run to the kid, hoist him up. Kid's like 'whatever' – does it all day. *Expects* to. Them grizzled old pricks in their dug out, they're lookin' at me, 'What was *that*?' I'm standing there *(folds his arms)*, 'It's called "football"' Ha ha! I tipped my hat – have some *brim* you cunts. He's a *surgeon* – he parts a defence like flesh. And he's *brave.* Eh? Heart of an ox. The kid is a *wonder.* The boy is a *lion.*

YATES I KNOW, JIM! I FOUND HIM!

Silence.

KIDD Eh?

What?

You...?

What?

YATES He came to me.

KIDD He *came* to you? Cos my understanding – I'm talking here what I've been *told*...you *found* him?

YATES Yes.

KIDD Cos my understanding is the kid walked in the door. Three months back, he walks in this door says he's looking for a club, who do I speak to for a *trial.* You're in here doing some *ironing* and you give him my phone number.

YATES I was waiting for him.

KIDD Excuse me?

YATES He walked in this door. *Someone* – he needed *someone* to be here.

KIDD He walks in the door you happen to *be* here?

YATES No.

KIDD Then *what*? Are you saying you prayed for him?

> *Pause.*

YATES I was here. He came. And I was here.

KIDD Huh. Hmm...fact is the boy *arrived*. And we can debate the manner of that 'coming' as we so please but let's agree he *showed up* – out of the wilderness say, clothed only in a – a – *loincloth*...

> **KIDD** *paces. Thinks. Stops. Gets it.*

Oh, you crazy fucking coot. On which planet do you have the *right*? You're managing him!

YATES Yes.

KIDD You work for *me*! You got no business getting into my player! There is a code carved in time's wall – YOU DON'T DO THAT!

> **YATES** *holds his ground.*

Has he signed something?

YATES No.

KIDD But you're his 'representative'?

YATES It's not official.

KIDD Are you *insane*?

YATES Don't think so.

KIDD You on the take?

YATES No.

KIDD You paying him?

YATES I help him out.

KIDD And you've told him not to sign his contract?

YATES Yes.

KIDD Well I hate to be a rat but I might have to tell the Board what you've been up to.

YATES *(scared)* Don't, Jim.

KIDD You've betrayed me and the club. 'Ledge.'

YATES *bows his head.*

You paying the boy to stroke your ego?

YATES *You* tried to pay him, six weeks back.

KIDD I didn't *pay* him, I slipped him thirty quid expenses!

YATES Which he *refused*!

KIDD *What*? He put the cash in his pocket! *Yeah.* He says, 'I can't take this, it's wrong.' I say, 'No it ain't, mate.' And he thinks and then he takes it, puts it in his pocket. He's a *kid* on the make. That's who *he* is. Why shouldn't he be?

YATES *is stunned.* **KIDD** *thinks a moment, turns.*

Roberts...how come you knew that Turner upped the offer?

You go back years with him. You fixed the deal – for Roberts!

YATES No! I'd never do that!

KIDD So what *did* you do? And don't lie, cos I'll know cos you sweat.

Pause.

YATES Robbo came to me.

KIDD Oh, they *all* come to you.

YATES He said he didn't wanna play for you no more. He wanted my advice. I put him in touch with Turner.

KIDD Instead of advising one of our best players to be loyal, you offered him to another club?

YATES *bows his head in shame.*

YATES *(softly)* I wanted Turner's respect. That I was still...

KIDD *Yeah.*

KIDD *stares at* **YATES** *with contempt.*

I'm off to the Board, all I care you can fuck off out this football club.

YATES For what? *Guiding* a player, *helping* a player?

KIDD For acting in contradiction to the interests of the football club. For disloyalty and disrespect to the appointed manager of this football club. For getting in the head of a valuable asset to this football club and filling said asset's head with fairy dust.

YATES Jim. Don't tell the Board. *Please.*

KIDD 'Please' don't cut it.

YATES *(begs)* This is all I got. It's all I got.

You know it. Let me sort it. I'll make it right.

KIDD You will make it *happen.* You will talk to your boy and get him to sign his contract – *now.* Or I'll go to the Board and you're finished here. You'll be disgraced.

YATES OK.

KIDD Off you go.

YATES *doesn't move. Thinking.*

Hello? Oh, screw it.

KIDD *puts his coat and hat on.*

You say your 'good-byes' to this room. I come back, you're *gone.*

KIDD *is about to exit.*

YATES Why was Tony Mac at the game?

Pause.

KIDD Who?

YATES Tony Mac.

KIDD Was he?

YATES You spoke after.

KIDD Don't think so.

YATES You and Tony Mac. Little chat out the car park.

KIDD Not me.

YATES I saw you. Him. And your hat.

KIDD So?

YATES He's a scout. Of sorts. A fixer. Well connected. A man you're desperate to impress. The man who can help you *rise*. He was here today...and he was here two weeks ago.

You want the boy on contract cos you've lied to Mac that he is.

Pause.

KIDD Good stab. Then what?

YATES You *need* him on contract so you and Mac can sell him. You want to sell the boy. At a price. You dirty fuck. You'll take a cut of the transfer fee, bung a bit to Mac. He'll do the same his end, shove some to you.

KIDD Sounds like a plan.

YATES It's what you *do*. You sell our children! You prefer to nick a few grand than keep a good player?

KIDD He was never gonna *stay*! Soon as he started *shining* we were never keeping him!

YATES *I* could keep him here!

KIDD It's not your business to!

YATES You don't even *want* to win the league?! We're *second*, we can win it!

KIDD Course I want to! Mac reckons we'll get twenny grand for him – it's a *gift* for the Board, buys me favour. Then I can get 'em to up the weekly – pay two or three new players. He's not the *difference*, I can win it without him.

YATES He's *our* player!

KIDD I gotta squad to look after. He makes 'em feel *ordinary* – bad for team spirit.

YATES The players love him!

KIDD NO, YOU DO! You got some *thing* going with him, thass sweet – thass fuckin' *weird* but no matter. This is a piece of *business*. The club acquires assets and sells or disposes of them as it deems appropriate. I *manage* that. It's my *job*. Your job is to wash and press the kit. Back in the day – your imagined day – all looking out for each other – *community* – cheers – this ain't that.

John. You drink too much. You think too much. You feel too much. I'm selling the player.

YATES (*furiously*) *NO!* You're in my club, this is *my* room!

The boy ain't going nowhere. He *belongs* here!

They face each other.

KIDD Nobody owns him, John.

YATES You go to the Board I come too. I'll tell 'em every crooked thing you do.

Pause.

KIDD Let's be gentlemen? Let's be sporting: we let *him* decide. He comes in we tell him the truth and we let him choose his future. Your way or mine.

YATES *considers the proposal.*

YATES Alright.

KIDD Done.

> **KIDD** *starts to undress to take a bath.* **YATES** *stands, thinking. Troubled.*

> Hang on. Why don't you *want* the kid on contract? Playing for the club you love?

> **YATES** *refuses to answer.* **KIDD** *shrugs, continues to undress.* **YATES** *stops, turns to* **KIDD**.

YATES I do want him on contract.

KIDD But?

YATES Not to you.

> *Pause.*

KIDD You never approved of me – day one – and I've *tried*. I came in two years back to a losing club, this was a morgue. Now we're buzzing. I give my all but it's never enough for you. The Ledge loves *everyone*...except me. Why? What've I gotta do?

> **KIDD** *is now stripped to his underwear.*

YATES Kiddo...

KIDD Say it. I'm a man. Why d'you hate me?

YATES Because you've got no manners. You never say 'please' or 'thank you'. You got a mouth like a potty. You've got the worst disciplinary record of any manager in this league. It *shames* us. You never notice the volunteers who make this club possible. You've got no interest in the *life* of the club. You corrupt the players. You rob them of their innocence. You're selfish. You're a liar. You're a user. So determined to get on you're not even here. Everywhere you go it ends ugly. You drive the club mad 'til it's a relief to pay you off. Anything to be rid of you. You're a thief, Jim. From a family of thieves and drunks. You did well to dodge the drink. You don't love this club or any club. You don't even love the game. You're the plague.

KIDD *smarts, wounded.*

KIDD That's clear.

He puts on his robe and exits to the bathroom. Sound of water running. Then, **KIDD** *re-enters, stands in the doorway. He stares at* **YATES** *while he works. After a while,* **YATES** *sees him and turns.*

I saw you play once. I was this...

He holds his hand three feet off the floor.

My dad brought me here. He was a cruel judge of a player. But now and then he'd come up here, just to watch *you*. No one else. He loved *you*. Any game, big game, nothing game...he said, 'You watch this feller driving his team on, you *notice* this man who would die out there. As if he longed for it. As if his life depends on the commitment he makes.' In our house, you were famous. Any of us, 'See, what you need more of, *boy*, what you need, *girl*, is the spirit *he's* got. You wanna *be* something in this world, go find in yourself what Johnny Yates is made of.'

When I was fifteen, I said, 'Dad, it's a lovely sentiment but you're an alcoholic postman. You're a depressed and disappointed pisshead who can't control himself.' He gave me a right old smack. And I was gone.

YATES Jim...

YATES *approaches but* **KIDD** *backs away and sits on a bench, head in hands.* **JORDAN** *enters wearing his club tracksuit.* **YATES** *gives him a look.* **JORDAN** *exits.*

I shouldn't have spoken.

KIDD I *asked* you. It's alright. I know what this job is. I got the courage to be despised. And I... John... I...am going places. All the way. I'm going there.

YATES Who's coming with you?

> **KIDD** *looks up at* **YATES**.

You don't have to be alone.

KIDD The manager handles it. Whatever it is. He stands apart. He's a *fort*. It's my job.

YATES No, it's your choice, Jim.

> *They look at each other.*

KIDD *(softly)* It's ever so lonely here.

YATES I've been there. You won't make it. No one can.

KIDD I will.

> **KIDD** *pulls himself together. Stands.*

You couldn't manage here – you couldn't *manage* – cos you're soft. You're a guy I inherited. You're a mascot. An old man I'm compelled to work with cos of history. I know your dream: you want me *out*. And then the Chairman says, 'John. In our hour of need, will you return and lead us to promotion, you and your sweet young Prince?'

And there it is: the *glory*.

Not in this life, pal.

> **KIDD** *heads to the bathroom.*

Your boy comes in you keep him here. And we will see where he stands.

> **KIDD** *exits to the bathroom. Turns the taps off, gets in the bath.* **YATES** *continues to tidy up. After a while,* **JORDAN** *enters.*

JORDAN OK?

YATES Yeah.

> **JORDAN** *nods to the bathroom.* **YATES** *nods.* **YATES** *goes to the fridge, takes out an ice pack from the freezer*

compartment, wraps it in a small towel, hands it to
JORDAN.

JORDAN Thanks.

JORDAN *sits on the bench, the ice pack held to his left*
knee.

YATES You speak to anyone after the game?

JORDAN No.

YATES No?

JORDAN Just a guy with Jimmy. Said I played well. Terry.

YATES Dark blue coat. Grey hair?

JORDAN Yeah. *Tony.* Jimmy said there were things we had to
talk about.

Pause.

YATES Why d'you take that money off him?

JORDAN *looks at* YATES.

JORDAN He wanted me to. I was scared.

YATES It gave him an in. He thinks you're biddable.

JORDAN It was thirty quid.

YATES I *told* you.

JORDAN You give me cash sometimes.

YATES *I'm* your guy, we're the team!

JORDAN I took his money *once.* I needed it.

YATES I bought you them boots. It's what I'm *here* for.

JORDAN *nods an apology.*

YATES Cos he's figured out our...thing.

JORDAN *looks at* YATES, *worried.*

JORDAN Am I in trouble?

YATES He doesn't blame you.

JORDAN Why would he?

YATES He doesn't.

JORDAN You said you'd look after me. Protect me. All the rest:
the contract, you and Jim – it's not my business. I just wanna
play. *(softly, sadly)* You think I'm something special. Want
me to be. But I ain't different class, John. I ain't all that.

YATES Yes you are.

JORDAN You wanna think it.

YATES I believe it.

JORDAN Don't make it true.

YATES You're good, son. *Believe.*

> **YATES** *makes his gesture of energy and uplift then stops
> himself.* **KIDD** *enters, towelling his hair.* **JORDAN** *conceals
> the ice pack.* **KIDD** *starts to get dressed. After a while:*

KIDD Ledge. Would you mind giving us a few minutes?

YATES No. We agreed we'd both talk to him.

KIDD *(to* **JORDAN***)* Your call.

> *Pause.*

JORDAN *(to* **YATES***)* I'll be alright.

YATES No. You won't.

> *Pause.*

JORDAN I'll find you if I'm not.

> **YATES** *stares at* **KIDD**.

KIDD He hath spoken.

> **YATES** *exits, humiliated.* **KIDD** *closes the door.*

You got yourself in a pickle there. S'alright. We've all done it.

He's a super fellow but he's got no business getting into you.

JORDAN But you're cool with him?

KIDD *Yeah*!

JORDAN It's alright?

KIDD It's gone!

JORDAN Cos I love that man.

KIDD I love him too. *Now*, we have a fast moving situation: you remember that guy? Tony Mac. Me and him have a number of arrangements. He's been talking to another guy at a big club – professional – sleeping giant, League One. And this club would like you to go up there for a trial.

JORDAN A trial?

KIDD Big step up. Well done you.

JORDAN What club?

KIDD A good and reputable club is all you need to know right now. And there are things it's best you *don't* know, I say this to protect you.

JORDAN Boss –

KIDD We need to establish some parameters for the deal – were it to happen.

JORDAN How would the trial work?

KIDD At present we're talking theoreticals.

JORDAN *Is* there a trial?

KIDD There *would* be – *if* me and you are in accord. Assuming we are you'd take a train to the Midlands and lodge with a kindly landlady for two weeks. You'd work with their first team squad. You'd do your lovely thing. A week or so later, all being well, they'd offer you a *contract*. Could be four hundred a week, maybe more. You would be a professional footballer. Bingo. A ticket to become someone *magical*. Don't forget your old chums.

JORDAN I – I can't afford the train fare or the landlady thing.

KIDD No, no, no, all the financing is my end.

JORDAN You?

KIDD It's not a thing. The thing – the pressing *thing* is we need you to sign your contract *here* so we can get a transfer fee. Without a contract they can sign you on a *free* and we, your friends, don't benefit. You see?

JORDAN Almost.

KIDD It's delicate. Now be a good lad and fetch your contract.

JORDAN *hesitates.*

JORDAN I should talk to John.

KIDD No, you can't talk to *him* cos you're talking to *me*. Get it. Please.

JORDAN *goes to his bag and finds the contract. He hands it to* KIDD.

Now to some people, a contract is a binding legal document.

JORDAN Isn't it?

KIDD I think of it as a chip. A position to come from. Its meaning is moot. And I'm not sure it has meaning in the strict sense of the word.

JORDAN What word?

KIDD The word 'meaning'.

JORDAN You want me to sign the contract and then break it?

KIDD He's got it.

JORDAN It don't sound right, Boss.

KIDD People say, 'You should not break a contract.' And yet and yet and yet, people *do*. The making and breaking of contracts is how life is *lived*. Property, finance, employment, legals, marriage. It's what we *do*. And by 'we' I think I mean the human species. So who is to say what's what in this world? Who are we to judge these people? Who are we to judge ourselves?

JORDAN It's complicated.

KIDD It is exactly that. So there are steps we must take and there may be subterfuge.

JORDAN But I like it here.

KIDD We like you for liking it.

JORDAN I like *playing* here. I love it.

KIDD Son. The Board have instructed me to sell you.

> JORDAN *reacts.*

It's not personal, they think you're *marvellous!* But the club needs the money. I've argued and raged, I can't win this one.

JORDAN Suppose I say no?

KIDD Then they'll stop your wage.

JORDAN I'll play for free?

KIDD No, no, no! Your worth in this world is what you *reap*. You don't play for zilch – I couldn't let you! You're *class*. Get what you *deserve*.

JORDAN But it's a Board meeting *now*, I could talk to 'em?

KIDD Nooo, you can't go in there!

> KIDD *barrs his way.* KIDD*'s phone rings. He scrambles for it. Answers.*

(in phone) Yeh. Now. Any second. Yeah!

> KIDD *puts the phone in his pocket.*

JORDAN Would they want me to have a medical?

KIDD Who?

JORDAN This other club.

KIDD Is that a problem?

JORDAN No.

KIDD You a cokehead? Cos they'll find that shit if you is.

JORDAN I don't do coke.

KIDD Of course you don't.

JORDAN The Midlands?

KIDD I know you have concerns. But let me walk you through the *maths* and you'll appreciate the upside.

JORDAN I dunno, Boss.

KIDD *Listen.* So, you trial and they like you. *Then* we can cut a little deal. You, me and them.

JORDAN A *deal*?

KIDD Mmm...

JORDAN About the fee?

KIDD Hmm?

JORDAN You're talking about the fee?

KIDD The fee?

JORDAN For the transfer?

KIDD No, no, no – something else. The fee is different, the club gets the fee.

JORDAN Which club?

KIDD *This* club, the selling club, who else?

JORDAN You said 'them' before.

KIDD When? Who?

JORDAN Just then, like a second ago.

KIDD Who said 'them'?

JORDAN You.

KIDD Me?

JORDAN *Yes.*

KIDD When?

JORDAN Just now!

KIDD I said 'them'?

JORDAN Yeah.

KIDD I don't think so. Huh. To tell you the truth I'm a bit lost here!

JORDAN I wanna talk to John. Can I talk to him, please?

KIDD He's gone home. You *can't* talk to him. He's not *entitled* to advise you. You talk to him the Board kick him out the club. Kill him. You don't want that.

JORDAN There's a fee and you said 'something else'.

KIDD There it is. Let's call it a bonus.

JORDAN Because it *is*?

KIDD Because let's call it that.

JORDAN This is fucked!

KIDD Oi! Sit *down* and *listen*!

JORDAN You fuck off, mister! I don't need your shit!

KIDD Yeah you do! Sit down and behave yourself! *This* is the conversation where you become a man who might amount to something.

Pause.

JORDAN What's the bonus for?

KIDD The bonus? Why it's a thank you.

JORDAN To you?

KIDD Me, you, everyone. Happy days.

JORDAN I don't –

KIDD It's a sweetener, common practice. Don't *fret*.

JORDAN I need to understand!

KIDD In actual fact, you really don't!

JORDAN Who are 'them'?

KIDD Fuck 'them' we're beyond that!

Pause.

JORDAN Do *I* get a bonus?

KIDD Yes you do, innit super? It's so super you don't wanna mention it. It's one of them great things best left unsaid.

Pause.

JORDAN How much?

KIDD The figure?

JORDAN Yeah.

KIDD Well it depends on the structure.

JORDAN Can't you just *tell* me? Tell me something I can *understand*!

KIDD There's a *number*. I suppose I could tell you that.

JORDAN OK.

KIDD The number is seven thousand pounds.

JORDAN No shit!

KIDD Innit sweet?!

JORDAN I get seven grand?!

KIDD Oh, I *wish*.

JORDAN But you said –

KIDD What did I say? I said that's the *number*. The *figure*, the figure is something else.

JORDAN The total is seven?

KIDD You see *this* is the conversation.

JORDAN Yeah. What do I get?

KIDD You get two and a half. Very tidy. Buy a car with that – you'll need it, zip off up the training ground each day.

JORDAN Who gets the rest?

KIDD It's really not relevant.

JORDAN *Who?*

KIDD 'Other parties to the deal.'

Pause.

JORDAN I want five.

KIDD It's not available.

JORDAN Five or forget it.

KIDD Five is not a conversation! Not worth our time you gonna fuck about all *naive*. See, me and Tony Mac we done the *work* here, set it up, for *you*.

JORDAN Is it legal?

KIDD Is that a serious question or something you're saying to pass the time?

JORDAN Is it legal?

KIDD Which?

JORDAN All of it – *any* of it?

KIDD I don't know, *is* it?

JORDAN I'm asking *you*!

KIDD Am I a lawyer?

JORDAN Is it *illegal*? Cos I ain't up for that.

Pause.

KIDD I know it's not *wrong*.

JORDAN Is it a bung?

KIDD No.

JORDAN What is it then?

KIDD It's *football*! It's how the poor survive! We're talking
'bout pocket money. The owner of this club, the big fat
builder, you know what he's *worth*? You think he cares?
We're underlings. *Atoms.* He bought the club so he could
sell the club. In five years he's gonna flog this ground to
the highest bidder. They'll build houses. And a superstore.
Councillers, planners, developers – all in it together, all
jolly old handshakes and Rotary Club. He'll make *millions.*
And then he'll make a few more when he builds this club
a crappy new (ha ha) 'community stadium' up near the
by-pass. A mean little ground made of breezeblock and
tin. And his company will *sponsor* it and *then* he'll launder
his cash through the club. It's the wild west down 'ere.
Unregulated. Every cunt for himself. It's a bleak English
landscape but there it is.

JORDAN I dunno.

KIDD You *need* to know cos everyone's *poised*. Would I fuck you?

JORDAN No.

KIDD Would I fuck myself?

JORDAN No.

KIDD So? You wanna stay *here*? Hundred quid a week and
part timers kicking lumps out you? Some scaffolder going
in studs up and the pissy blind shitbag ref never noticing
fuck all – the elbows and the knees and the fist in your
bollocks? Crappy pitches and cold showers and a Tesco
sausage roll after the game? *(Passionately)* God gave you
brilliance – and now you've got an *out* – TAKE IT! You've
earned it, you *deserve* it! Your past – what you run from –
whatever dark thing drives you – you can *escape*! There is
nothing here. You get the fuck out this place boy and don't
ever look back. I want this deal, feller. I ain't gonna lie,

I need it – for reasons I hope you never know. But it also happens I want to save your life.

JORDAN Why?

KIDD Because it's worth saving. Because it *can* be saved. Sign this contract here and now – give yourself a future.

JORDAN I gotta talk to the Ledge.

Pause.

KIDD He knows.

He knows enough. Don't talk to him. You talk to him he's involved. You understand?

JORDAN *stares. Desolate.*

JORDAN Does he get a cut?

KIDD He gets a little slice.

Pause.

JORDAN He's cool with it?

KIDD Yeah.

JORDAN ...Huh...

Pause.

KIDD You see?

JORDAN *nods, devastated.*

He's *happy* for you, just can't say it. He set you on your way. Now you're saying 'thank you'.

JORDAN He wants me out the club.

KIDD No! He wants you to prosper, to progress. He wants what's best for you. This was always an option, day you walked in this door. It's good for everyone, it's really not a thing.

KIDD *offers a pen.*

The guy's waiting for my word. You're gonna sign this and get up there tomorrow. And who knows? They might be stupid, might not fancy ya. So you come back here and... we'll do something else.

JORDAN I can't play here, you want me out.

KIDD Don't you get it, you're too good for us!

JORDAN *John* wants me out, he lied to me.

KIDD Hey. Don't be too hard on the old boy.

You're talking about a – a decent man.

And...he ain't all there, you know?

Twenny years ago. When he was the boss...he took this club down...and he...well, he lost his way. That season. He couldn't cope.

He lost his marriage, his kids. They moved abroad. They're in New Zealand. He lost his home. All gone. And then he's on the street. He was a...homeless. You know?

And he vanishes. Goes missing. For ten years. *Ten* years.

Then he turns up one night. Some hostel in Carlisle. He's all beaten. Can't talk. He's *gone*.

They say, 'D'you know your name?'

All he does is roar. He just...*roars*.

So they calm him...*shhh*...they feed him and they hose him down...

And they see he's got a tattoo on his heart. A Red Lion. The club crest. This badge.

They call. And three old boys from the Supporters Club, they go up there and bring him back.

And very slowly, he recovers his marbles...and in time, they let him manage the kit.

So you go easy on that feller.

Cos he's been around.

56

THREE

Two weeks later. Night.

YATES *stands alone. In his coat. Under it a shirt and tie. He takes in the room. It's clean and tidy.* **KIDD**'s *hat is on a hook.* **YATES** *pulls a bottle of beer from his coat pocket, smacks it open at the sink. Drinks.*

He stares at the room.

KIDD *enters. They look at each other.*

KIDD You killed me.

Pause.

YATES Had to do it.

KIDD Why?

YATES Had to be rid of you.

KIDD Why?

YATES I love the club.

KIDD You *love*?

YATES I love this football club.

KIDD They just let you *go*!

YATES I was disloyal.

KIDD You're finished!

YATES It's a Board decision. I accept it.

YATES *goes to his cupboard and opens it. Stuff tumbles out. A ball, pumps, cones, etc.* **YATES** *lets them fall.*

KIDD Where you gonna go?

YATES *rummages and pulls out an old kit bag. He searches some more in the cupboard and pulls out his boots, an old trophy, some medals, a framed photo, a soft toy lion. He stuffs them in the bag.*

What you gonna *do*, John?

YATES *closes the cupboard leaving the key in the lock.*

KIDD That *kid*.

YATES Yeah.

KIDD Did you *know*?

YATES No.

YATES *goes to his kit bag. Finds a screwdriver. He heads over to his peg and attempts to unscrew it from the wall. It won't budge.* **YATES** *sweats with the effort.*

KIDD He's in there now.

YATES *looks blank.*

In the Board room. I came out he's going in.
(softly) He fucked us.
And now he'll fuck me some more.

YATES *has another go at the peg.*

Did you have to tell 'em *everything*?

YATES I answered their questions.

KIDD Loyalty!

YATES I know.

KIDD The dressing room. IT STAYS IN HERE! It's the only law!

YATES I didn't volunteer the information. It's a disciplinary. Club business. We misbehaved. We've been punished.

KIDD They've suspended me.

'Pending further investigation into a series of gross misconducts.' Something like that.

I'm banned from the ground. I'm...*suspended*... I can't do a thing.

I'm off the *premises*...

Banished.

I'm not allowed to *talk* to my players. I can't *talk* to a club employee.

Who am I gonna talk to?

YATES You can talk to me.

KIDD *(softly)* They said I'm a crook. In some respects it's not untrue. But Jesus, I'm small fry. Chairman said a thing about *fraud*, get police involved.

YATES Get a lawyer.

KIDD I said, 'Guys, I can't *live* on what you're paying me. Few hundred a week. It can't be *done*, I gotta work the angles.'

KIDD *looks out the window, anxiously.*

John. I put a brick through the Chairman's window. I just smashed his car. I wish I hadn't. There's cameras out there. I fucked myself.

KIDD *watches* **YATES** *struggling.*

What are you doing?

YATES I want my peg.

KIDD Fuck sake.

KIDD *watches the struggle some more.*

Here.

YATES *hands him the screwdriver.* **KIDD** *has a go. He grunts with the effort.*

KIDD Ancient frickin' things. Some cock painted over the screws.

YATES So he did.

> **KIDD** *keeps trying.*

KIDD I'm gonna try chip the paint off.

YATES Good thinking.

KIDD I'm gonna chip it off with *this*.

> **KIDD** *works at the paint with the screwdriver. He tries the screws again. Struggles.*

> *(grunting to heaven)* Will you grant me the gift of some purchase?

> **KIDD** *finally gets some movement.*

> It's coming! It's turning! Yeeaasss!

> **KIDD** *manages to wrench off the peg – but a screw cuts his hand as he pulls it off.*

> Shit!!

> *He hands the peg to* **YATES**.

YATES Thank you.

> **KIDD** *holds his hand up, the blood flows, he heads to the sink to rinse the cut.*

KIDD I'm cut. I'm wounded. I'm bleeding...ooh...haahh...don't like my blood... John...?

> **KIDD** *is unsteady, could faint.* **YATES** *helps him over to the treatment table, sits him down, raises* **KIDD**'s *arm above his head.* **YATES** *fetches medical supplies. He starts to clean up the wound.*

> Hey...go back in there? Help me. Tell 'em...tell the Board...

YATES Tell 'em what?

KIDD I lose this job. I'm out the game. You get done for 'gross' you're *tarnished.* Ruined. I've got children.

YATES *wraps a bandage round the wound.*

John. D'you miss your kids?

YATES ...Yeah...

YATES *ties off the bandage.*

KIDD I *like* you. Why d'you take against me? We had some laughs. Had some...moments. Thoughts. Tactics. Three weeks back, we were hugging on the touchline.

YATES You want a hug, Jim?

KIDD *Please.* Go back in there? Tell 'em they're wrong. Tell 'em...we're top of the league.

YATES *stares at* **KIDD,** *then looks out at the pitch.*

YATES *(distantly)* I think of those men...a dozen men in a room above 'The Red Lion'. In 1892. They founded a football club. Not for profit, not to further their standing in the town but to meet a need; that a crowd of people gathered together in support of a team has purpose. *Meaning.*

The game is ritual; made up rules, man made oppositions. Make believe.

The *crowd,* the ceremony, the collusion of souls *willing* it to matter – makes it matter. This will never happen again. Not like *this.*

Something so pure, so innocent, we forget we have it.

Those men knew. They knew we would need to *yearn* for the sacred.

You and men like you. You sold out our clubs and you sold out our game.

KIDD I *love* this game! It's my *life* ya pompous old prick! People *like* the mess of it – they like the biting and fighting and greed – it's *human*!!! It's not *church.* It's not merry old

'Association Football'. It's a *business* and nothing – nothing I know in this world stops money. Five, six years they will *raze* your stand. Bulldoze it. You gonna protest on the pitch? You gonna plant yourself there with Ken and Joan and the Supporter's Club? All waving the club's code of conduct like King Canute?

YATES *(distantly)* I'm just a man. I am weak. Give me your strength.

KIDD John, don't go mad, wake up, come the fuck back to earth and *spare* me! Go back in there. *Fight* for me. We belong together. Ain't no one else gonna front up for me. I can't *retrain*, I can't work for some *company* – I don't wear a logo – I wear this *badge*! I've got no trade, I'm an idiot, I'm *this*. I live in *here* and out *there* on that beautiful fucking meadow. There's nothing else.

JORDAN *comes in.*

JORDAN *(to* **KIDD***)* They wanna see you.

KIDD Again?

JORDAN Yeah.

KIDD *Now?*

JORDAN Yes.

KIDD What d'you tell 'em? What *didn't* you tell 'em?

YATES Jim. Remember you're an adult.

KIDD *(to* **JORDAN***)* Piece of fucking shit!

JORDAN You shut your mouth!

KIDD You fucking Judas!

JORDAN *approaches* **KIDD.**

JORDAN You wanna say that again?

KIDD No cos I've said it already!

JORDAN *approaches.* KIDD *picks up the screwdriver.*
Brandishes it.

JORDAN Oh, thass cool.

KIDD Ledge, you gonna call him off? John? Yatesy?!

JORDAN *grabs* KIDD*'s arm and twists it behind his back,*
takes the screwdriver.

Aaarrgghhh!

JORDAN *tortures* KIDD *for a few seconds.* KIDD *squeals*
in pain. JORDAN *pulls* KIDD *on to the treatment table,*
pins him down. His capacity for violence is extreme.
JORDAN *raises the screwdriver – murderously – to stab*
KIDD *in the face.*

YATES *(to* JORDAN*)* Don't! He's beaten. No need to kill him.
Son. Let him go.

After a few moments, JORDAN *lets* KIDD *go.* JORDAN
looks from KIDD *to* YATES.

JORDAN You two! You messed with my head!

KIDD Excuse me? *What*?! Me and him are out the club cos
of *you*!

JORDAN Yeah me too – and I'm sorry – but it ain't my *fault*!

KIDD Not your *fault*? Did we force you to go up to the Midlands
with a knee full of steroids? Did we inject that shit you been
using to manage the pain?

JORDAN You both got right in *here*!

KIDD Might you not – as a *Christian* – have found it in your
good Godly heart to confess to your colleagues that you
couldn't go on a trial cos your leg is swimming with anabolic
goat piss?!

JORDAN I couldn't think – I lost my way!

KIDD You take a medical you think they ain't gonna *find* it?! You *case*!

JORDAN I hoped they might fix it!

KIDD Your knee is fucked, boy!

JORDAN I didn't know how much!

KIDD Find a new sport – *snooker*! You keep shooting that shit you won't walk when you're thirty!

JORDAN I hoped they might want me enough to *help* me!

KIDD But they didn't!

JORDAN I hoped they might find me a specialist who could –

KIDD They were angry you wasted their time! They were perplexed – understandably – that the parent club (us) sent them a *cripple* posing as a player! They called our chairman and then they lodged a formal complaint with the FA. You worked a miracle; you stirred our Board to convene a series of emergency meetings. First time they've acted with urgency for a hundred years. You and your gammy leg have brought this club into disrepute. They'll get fined, it'll be in the *Herald*, it's *bad*. You've made us look like amateurs.

JORDAN You *are*! Those guys up there – different league!

KIDD Fuck off! OK, we don't do drugs tests but we know our stuff, me and him.

JORDAN No, you really *don't*! Those men, they were *pro*. They know this game; the drills and the training, systems, moves, options, fitness, nutrition. You people here – *Old Testament*! They don't tell me to dive, nor give you some cash and think they *own* you. They're professional people!

KIDD You *lied* to us from day one! *(To* **YATES***)* How can you bear this?

YATES I admit, it's disappointing.

JORDAN *(To* YATES*)* Yeah? You sad you don't get your *cut*? Your little slice?

YATES *is confused. Looks at* KIDD *who plays innocent.*

He said you were in on it…?

YATES *(to* KIDD*)* You told him I was on the take?

Pause.

KIDD Yeah. I know, it's not impressive.

JORDAN *(to* YATES*)* You weren't?

YATES No.

YATES *stares at* KIDD.

KIDD Yes you *were*. You took him from me. You took my boy.

YATES *(to* KIDD*)* Don't keep the Board waiting.

KIDD *takes a look round the room, goes to the mirror, straightens his tie.*

KIDD They're gonna fire me. Right now. *I* would.

I think…hmm…sometimes get a bit above myself. Oh…shit…

KIDD *wipes his eyes.* YATES *opens his arms.*

YATES You'll survive.

KIDD No I won't.

YATES You cheer up now.

KIDD Oh, I'm cheerful.

YATES Always restless. Can't stop to think.

KIDD If I think I'll die.

YATES Have a drink.

KIDD I'm teetotal.

YATES Have a cuddle.

KIDD No thanks.

YATES You ever had a cuddle?

KIDD Never.

YATES No?

KIDD Proud of it.

YATES Not your old mum? Your dad?

KIDD Fuck off.

YATES Couldn't do it, eh?

KIDD I don't remember.

YATES You don't recall it?

KIDD No, mate.

YATES Kids need a cuddle, *all* kids need a little cuddle.

KIDD *I* didn't.

YATES D'you cuddle your kids?

James.

Jimmy Kidd.

Do you love your children?

Have you ever loved a single living soul?

For a while, **KIDD** *stands, inconsolable. Then, he gets it together.*

KIDD They fire me, fuck 'em. I done it before I'll do it again: kids team, youth team, pub team, Sunday league, County league, step step step – I'm back.

I am *good* at this game.

KIDD *starts to exit.*

YATES Kiddo. Your hat.

KIDD *stops. Takes his hat from the hook.* **KIDD** *holds the hat, looks at* **JORDAN**.

KIDD I loved watching you play. Good luck to you.

JORDAN nods. **KIDD** *puts the hat on.*

John. You killed me. But I forgive you.

YATES Thank you, Jim.

Then slowly, respectfully, **KIDD** *doffs his hat to* **YATES**.
KIDD *exits.*

JORDAN I let you down. I shoulda told you I was injured. I needed to play.

YATES *nods, understanding.*

Jimmy said...you went right under. Was that true?

YATES Yeah.

YATES *thinks a moment and then hands his peg to* **JORDAN**.

YATES Would you put this back for me?

JORDAN *takes the peg over to the wall and starts to screw it back on.* **YATES** *turns away, stares out at the pitch.*

JORDAN I got off the train today. At Euston. And I was certain, 'Go missing. Never be seen again.' I couldn't face you. Couldn't face no one. I couldn't bear this life. I lay outside the station. On the grass. And I imagined it, a long time. Escape.

JORDAN *has finished the peg.* **YATES** *nods his thanks.*

I came home and my mum got herself a new man. They are *doing* it. I'm movin' out. I ain't listening to that.

YATES Mmm.

JORDAN You know?

YATES There is no more appalling sound. Reminds us where we came from.

Was it your father, broke your leg?

JORDAN *nods.*

I asked too much of you. I needed too much. All heart. No touch.

Pause.

JORDAN You gonna look for another club?

YATES *shakes his head. He goes to the sink, washes his face.*

You should. You got knowledge. Up there I was thinking, 'I wish John was here. He'd know the drill. He'd fit in.'

YATES *(softly, distantly)* When I was born.

My mum brought me to the match.

They said, here's a young Lion.

After the game, after a drink...

They brought me up here. Bathed me.

YATES *dries his hands.*

I could play a bit...

Way back when...

YATES *stares at the room.*

This dreaming game...

Seven years old.

Here are my knees...

My boots...

A goal...

I remember.

The sound.

Booof...

Silence.

A cheer.

Is this it? That thing?

Yes! Turning away. Reeling.

Arm in the air, one arm in the air, like my father, like the men I revered, my arm raised, wheeling with joy.

Running, running...

I ghost through me.

Vanishing child...

Seven.

To be free.

To be a boy.

Greatness...

Oh.

How would that be?

They look at each other.

I'll miss the floodlights.

The grass and the boys.

Such light.

You like an evening game?

JORDAN I love 'em.

YATES *approaches* JORDAN. *Kisses his forehead.*

YATES Look after yourself.

JORDAN Always.

Pause.

If I can play again...can I let you know?

YATES *nods.*

Will you come and watch me?

YATES I'll watch you.

Pause.

JORDAN See you on the park.

JORDAN *exits.*

YATES *takes a swig from his bottle of beer.*

He gazes out at the pitch.

And then murmurs his chant, slowly, softly...

YATES Johnny Yates...

Johnny Yates...

Johnny, Johnny Yates...

He's a lion...

Made of iron...

Johnny...

Johnny...

Yates.

End

PROPERTY LIST

ACT ONE

Single bag, contains washbag with toothbrush and paste	p1
Black trench coat	p1
Iron, ironing board, laundry basket containing 16 match day shirts numbered 1-17, no '13'	p1
Sixteen hanger	p1
Tube of shower gel, mobile phone (**KIDD**)	p1
Key (**YATES**)	p1
Suit in cupboard with tie in jacket pocket (**KIDD**)	p2
Shorts and socks x16	p5
Broom (**YATES**)	p6
Dustpan and brush (**YATES**)	p7
Massage oils and lotions	p9
Kit bag (**JORDAN**)	p10
Twenty match day programmes (**YATES**)	p14
Club tracksuit and kit bag	p14
Towels	p15
Laundry basket	p25
Mop and packet of Rich Tea biscuits (**YATES**)	p27
Syringe and phial (**JORDAN**)	p27

ACT TWO

Dirty kit on the floor, empty plastics bottles, shin pads, sock tape, bandages and a subs board	p28
Cheap phone (**KIDD**)	p28
Pint, wrapped bag of chips with a saveloy (**YATES**)	p28
Ketchup	p29
Three baskets	p29
Can of Diet Coke	p30
Ice pack	p43
Contract	p47

ACT THREE

Bottle of beer (**YATES**)	p56
Ball, pumps, cones etc in cupboard	p56
Old kit bag, books, old trophy, medals, framed photo and soft toy lion	p57
Screwdriver	p57
Medical supplies	p59

COSTUME

Act One
YATES – club tracksuit and trainers, initials JY in white letters
on the track top.
KIDD – flip-flops, white bathrobe

Act Two
KIDD – black trench coat over suit and fedora
YATES – coat over tracksuit

SOUND

From offstage, sound of a shower running   p1

VISIT THE SAMUEL FRENCH BOOKSHOP AT THE ROYAL COURT THEATRE

Browse plays and theatre books, get expert advice and enjoy a coffee

Samuel French Bookshop
Royal Court Theatre
Sloane Square
London
SW1W 8AS
020 7565 5024

Shop from thousands of titles on our website

 samuelfrench.co.uk

 samuelfrenchltd

 samuel french uk